M000081817

living with loss

dedication

To Ellen, Chelsea, and Liane,
and in loving memory of Melvin.

Published by Sellers Publishing, Inc.
Copyright © 2014 Sellers Publishing, Inc.
Photography copyright © 2014 Steven N. Meyers
All rights reserved.

Credits appear on page 64.

Sellers Publishing, Inc.
161 John Roberts Road, South Portland, Maine 04106
www.sellerspublishing.com • E-mail: rsp@rsvp.com
ISBN 13: 978-1-4162-4507-0

10 9 8 7 6 5 4 3 2 1
Printed and bound in China.

living with loss

keep hope close to your heart ...

compiled by Robin Haywood

photography by Steven N. Meyers

SELLERS

PUBLISHING

Rose
broken heart

The loss of a loved one
is like the loss of a part of oneself;
an arm or a leg.
At first, the pain is so physical
that it is hard to ignore.
The trauma is so intense
that the mind finds it hard to cope
with the loss. With time the pain eases,
the body recovers, and the brain figures out
new ways to go on.

Federico Chini

The most beautiful people
I've known are those
who have known trials,
have known struggles,
have known loss,
and have found their way
out of the depths.

Elisabeth Kübler-Ross

Hyacinth
sorrow

I guess by now
I should know enough about loss
to realize that you never
really stop missing someone,
you just learn to live
around the huge gaping hole
of their absence.

Alyson Noel

Cyclamen
good-bye

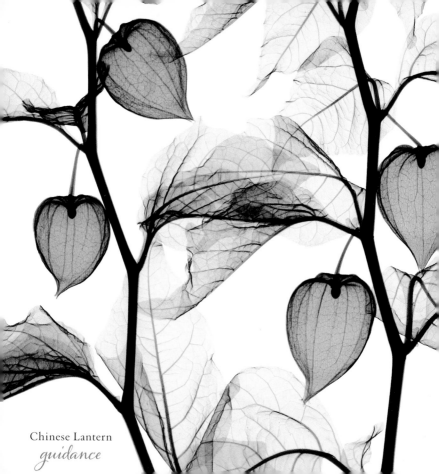

Chinese Lantern
guidance

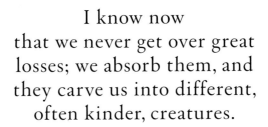

I know now
that we never get over great
losses; we absorb them, and
they carve us into different,
often kinder, creatures.

Gail Caldwell

Anemone
eternal love

It's only after we've
lost everything
that we're free
to do anything.

Chuck Palahniuk

I sit quietly and think about my mom.
It's funny how memory erodes.
If all I had to work from
were my childhood memories,
my knowledge of my mother
would be faded and soft,
with a few sharp memories
standing out.

Audrey Niffenegger

Hydrangea
remembrance

Lily and buds
devotion

It's so much darker
when a light goes out
than it would have been
if it had never shone.

John Steinbeck

I am told many children

block out the memory of trauma.

In fact, the healing process

can only truly begin

when we are willing

to remember.

Phoebe Stone

Triumph Tulip
memory

Chrysanthemum
precious one

She had been grief stricken
as her father lay dying
but now she felt weightless,
the way people do when they're no longer
sure they have a reason to be connected
to this world. The slightest breeze
could have carried her away,
into the night sky, across the universe.

Alice Hoffman

Suffering invites us to place our hurts
in larger hands. In Christ we see God
suffering — for us, and calling us to share
in His suffering love for a hurting world.
The small and even overpowering pains of
our lives are intimately connected with the
greater pains of Christ. Our daily sorrows
are anchored in a greater sorrow and
therefore a larger hope.

Henri J. M. Nouwen

Passion Vine
faith

Dogwood
durability

In the hero stories, the call to go on a journey
takes the form of a loss, an error, a wound,
an unexplainable longing, or a sense of
a mission. When any of these happens to us,
we are being summoned to make a transition.
It will always mean leaving something behind. . . .
The paradox here is that loss is a path to gain.

David Richo

If there were no life beyond this earth-life,

some people I have known would gain immortality

by the nobility of our memory of them.

With every friend I love who has been taken

into the brown bosom of the earth,

a part of me has been buried there;

but their contribution of happiness, strength,

and understanding to my being remains

to sustain me in an altered world.

Helen Keller

Calla Lily
rebirth

Lily Muscadet
devotion

There has not been a day since his sudden and mysterious vanishing that I have not been searching for him, looking in the most unlikely places. Everything and everyone, existence itself, has become an evocation, a possibility for resemblance. Perhaps this is what is meant by that brief and now almost archaic word: elegy.

Hisham Matar

"*I think,*" Tehanu said in her soft, strange voice,
"*that when I die, I can breathe back the breath*
that made me live. I can give back to the world
all that I didn't do. All that I might have been
and couldn't be. All the choices I didn't make.
All the things I lost and spent and wasted.
I can give them back to the world.
To the lives that haven't been lived yet.
That will be my gift back to the world
that gave me the life I did live,
the love I loved, the breath I breathed."

Ursula K. Le Guin

Poppy
eternal sleep

Carnation
never forget

"She heard him mutter,
'Can you take away this grief?'

"*'I'm sorry,'* she replied.
*'Everyone asks me. And I would not do
so even if I knew how. It belongs to you.
Only time and tears take away grief;
that is what they are for.'*"

Terry Pratchett

"I'll cry with you," she whispered,
*"until we run out of tears. Even if it's forever.
We'll do it together."*

There it was . . . a simple promise
of connection. The loving alliance
of grief and hope that blesses
both our breaking apart
and our coming together again.

Molly Fumia

Parrot Tulip
forever love

Canterbury Bells
gratitude

. . . our loved ones truly are ever present. We may bury their bodies or scatter their ashes, but their spirits are boundless and do not accompany them to the grave. The terms "letting go" and "closure" are just empty words. They mean nothing to someone who has suffered through the death of a loved one. Instead of insisting on figuratively burying our dead, why not keep them close to us?

Love doesn't die when we do.

April Slaughter

It was a fine cry — loud and long —
but it had no bottom and it had no top,
just circles and circles of sorrow.

Toni Morrison

Dahlia
dignity

Hyacinth
sorrow

Everyone keeps telling me that time heals all wounds, but no one can tell me what I'm supposed to do right now. Right now I can't sleep. It's right now that I can't eat. Right now I still hear his voice and sense his presence even though I know he's not here. Right now all I seem to do is cry. I know all about time and wounds healing, but even if I had all the time in the world, I still don't know what to do with all this hurt right now.

Nina Guilbeau

I cried until my eyes
swelled shut, and then I slept,
a black, dreamless sleep from
which I awoke amazingly
refreshed, at least until
I remembered.

Elizabeth Berg

Poppy
eternal sleep

Lily buds
devotion

She was brave
from excess
of grief.

Edith Hamilton

"I lost a child," she said, meeting Lusa's eyes directly. *"I thought I wouldn't live through it. But you do. You learn to love the place somebody leaves behind for you."*

Barbara Kingsolver

Iris

faith and hope

Anemone
unfading love

Every one of us is losing something
precious to us. Lost opportunities,
lost possibilities, feelings we can
never get back again. That's part of
what it means to be alive.

Haruki Murakami

She felt the depth of her losses before they were realized, and she wondered, Is there still hope? Did she even dare hold on to such a tenuous thing as hope?

Sage Steadman

Plumeria
shelter

Eucalyptus
protection

Deep grief sometimes is almost like a specific location, a coordinate on a map of time. When you are standing in that forest of sorrow, you cannot imagine that you could ever find your way to a better place. But if someone can assure you that they themselves have stood in that same place, and now have moved on, sometimes this will bring hope.

Elizabeth Gilbert

"Lost love is still love, Eddie. It just takes a different form, that's all. You can't hold their hand. . . . You can't tousle their hair . . . . But when those senses weaken another one comes to life. Memory. Memory becomes your partner. You hold it . . . you dance with it. . . . Life has to end, Eddie. Love doesn't."

Mitch Albom

Lily and bud
love

Amaryllis
poetry

(on grief) And you do come out of it, that's true. After a year, after five. But you don't come out of it like a train coming out of a tunnel, bursting through the downs into sunshine and that swift, rattling descent to the Channel; you come out of it as a gull comes out of an oil-slick. You are tarred and feathered for life.

Julian Barnes

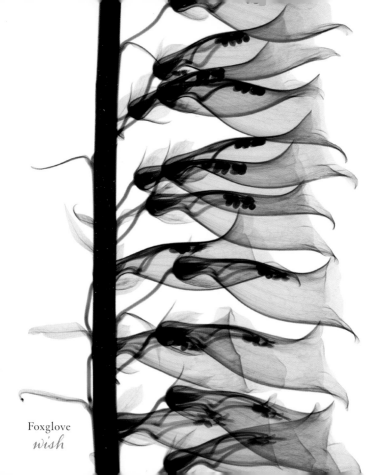

Foxglove
wish

You will lose someone you can't live without,
and your heart will be badly broken, and the bad
news is that you never completely get over the loss
of your beloved. But this is also the good news.
They live forever in your broken heart
that doesn't seal back up. And you come through.
It's like having a broken leg that never
heals perfectly — that still hurts
when the weather gets cold,
but you learn to dance with the limp.

Anne Lamott

"It was too perfect to last," so I am tempted to say of our marriage. But it can be meant in two ways. It may be grimly pessimistic — as if God no sooner saw two of His creatures happy than He stopped it ("None of that here!"). As if He were like the hostess at the sherry-party who separates two guests the moment they show signs of having got into a real conversation. But it could also mean "This had reached its proper perfection. This had become what it had in it to be. Therefore of course it would not be prolonged." As if God said, "Good; you have mastered that exercise. I am very pleased with it. And now you are ready to go on to the next."

C. S. Lewis

Allium
unity

Daffodil

respect

In sorrow we must go, but not in despair.

Behold! we are not bound forever to the

circles of the world, and beyond them

is more than memory.

J. R. R. Tolkien

Credits:

p. 5 Federico Chini, from *The Sea of Forgotten Memories*; p. 6 Elisabeth Kübler-Ross; p. 8 Alyson Noel, from *Evermore*; p. 11 Gail Caldwell, from *Let's Take the Long Way Home: A Memoir of Friendship*; p. 13 Chuck Palahniuk, from *Fight Club*; p. 14 Audrey Niffenegger, from *The Time Traveler's Wife*; p. 17 John Steinbeck, from *The Winter of Our Discontent*; p. 18 Phoebe Stone, from *The Boy on Cinnamon Street*; p. 21 Alice Hoffman, from *Skylight Confessions*; p. 22 Henri J. M. Nouwen; p. 25 David Richo, form *How to Be an Adult: A Handbook on Psychological and Spiritual Integration*; p. 26 Helen Keller, from *The Open Door*; p. 29 Hisham Matar, from *Anatomy of a Disappearance*; p. 30 Ursula K. Le Guin, from *The Other Wind*; p. 33 Terry Pratchett, from *I Shall Wear Midnight*; p. 34 Molly Fumia, from *Safe Passage*; p. 37 April Slaughter, from *Reaching Beyond the Veil*; p. 38 Toni Morrison, from *Sula*; p. 41 Nina Guilbeau, from *Too Many Sisters*; p. 42 Elizabeth Berg, from *The Year of Pleasures*; p. 45 Edith Hamilton, from *Mythology*; p. 46 Barbara Kingsolver, from *Prodigal Summer*; p. 49 Haruki Murakami, from *Kafka on the Shore*; p. 50 Sage Steadman, from *Upon Destiny's Song*; p. 53 Elizabeth Gilbert, from *Eat, Pray, Love*; p. 54 Mitch Albom; p. 57 Julian Barnes, from *Flaubert's Parrot*; p. 59 Anne Lamott; p. 60 C. S. Lewis, from *A Grief Observed*; p. 63 J. R. R. Tolkien.